"DO ONE THING EVERY DAY

ON THE FIRST PAGE

of this book, the thirteenth-century Persian poet and mystic Rumi calls across space and time. And you? When will you begin that long journey into yourself?" On the last page, the contemporary American rapper and songwriter Nas shouts from a billboard in Times Square, "The further I get, the further I want to go." Although *Do One Thing Every Day That Centers You* is a journal of unnumbered pages, meant to be flipped through and dipped back into throughout the year, these two quotes are appropriate bookends.

In between them are words of inspiration and prompts for everyday acts to help you move inward and onward toward a centered life. The insights of writers, poets, athletes, actors, scientists, entrepreneurs, artists, presidents, novelists, saints, philosophers, and gurus are matched with daily prompts to help you grow in heart, mind, body, and spirit. There are also pages with activities to expand your awareness and appreciation; ways to gauge your path to self understanding; and exercises to calm, open, and stretch yourself, both literally and figuratively.

The word *centers* in its use today, and even in the title of this book, is a slippery one,

THAT CENTERS YOU."

often defined by other intangible terms—mindfulness, gratitude, wholeness, groundedness, focus, flow, serenity, self-knowledge, and self-acceptance. The best definition, however, comes not from the heady realm of ideas, but from the hands-on world of craft. Every potter knows how difficult it is to learn how to center clay on a wheel. It takes hours and hours and days and days of dedication and practice, until your hands "know" the clay well enough to center it. If you move ahead too early, your pot will be unsteady, fragile, and unattractive. But once you find the center, your pot—whatever your personal desire and design for it—will be balanced, secure, and beautiful.

For most people, creating a centered life, like molding that pot, requires dedication and practice. The quotes in this journal aim to provide inspiration and guidance. As you reflect on them, respond to them, and complete the related activities, you will come to know the power of giving and receiving, of friendship and community. You will be urged to expand your knowledge and to edge it toward wisdom. You will appreciate the places, people, and experiences that give peace to your body and meaning to your life. When you are ready, breathe in and breathe out, turn the page—and **BEGIN!**

AND YOU?
WHEN WILL
YOU BEGIN
THAT LONG
JOURNEY INTO
YOURSELF?

Rūmī

TODAY! How?

_____

_____

_____

Might, could, would— they are contemptible auxiliaries.

George Eliot

Today I will:

_____

_____

_____

I make
the most of all
that comes
and the least
of all
that goes.

Sara Teasdale

DATE: __/__/__

I MADE THE MOST OF THIS TODAY:

_____

_____

_____

_____

_____

_____

DATE: __/__/__

I MADE THE LEAST OF THIS TODAY:

_____

_____

_____

_____

_____

_____

WHAT WE HAVE TO LEARN TO DO, WE LEARN BY DOING.

Aristotle

What I learned by doing today:

_____

_____

_____

Friendship is unnecessary, like philosophy, like art, like the universe itself.... It has no survival value; rather it is one of those things which give value to survival.

C. S. Lewis

How a friend gave value to my survival today:

_____

_____

_____

The simple things in nature that bring me pleasure:

_____

_____

_____

_____

_____

_____

One impulse from a vernal wood
May teach you more of man,
Of moral evil and of good,
Than all the sages can.

William Wordsworth

What I learned from nature today:

_____

_____

_____

DATE: _/_/_

Shall we make a new rule of life from tonight: always try to be a little kinder than is necessary?

James M. Barrie

How I was a little kinder than necessary today:

_____

_____

_____

THERE ARE NO TRAFFIC JAMS ALONG THE EXTRA MILE.

Roger Staubach

How I went the extra mile today:

_____

_____

_____

The only ones among you who will be really happy are those who will have sought and found how to serve.

Albert Schweitzer

How I served today:

_____

_____

_____

AS WE EXPRESS OUR GRATITUDE, WE MUST NEVER FORGET THAT THE HIGHEST APPRECIATION IS NOT TO UTTER WORDS, BUT TO LIVE BY THEM.

John F. Kennedy

Words I lived by today:

_____

_____

_____

THE WISE,
FOR CURE,
ON EXERCISE
DEPEND.

John Dryden

Exercise, mental or physical, that cured me today:

_____

_____

_____

DATE: __/__/__

I don't count my sit-ups; I only start counting when it starts hurting . . . because then it really counts.

Muhammad Ali

Number of _____s that counted today:

_____

_____

_____

S-T-R-E-T-C-H

**I STRETCHED MY MIND TODAY BY
LEARNING SOMETHING SCIENTIFIC:**

_____

_____

_____

_____

_____

_____

_____

DATE: __/__/__

YOUR M-I-N-D

I STRETCHED MY MIND TODAY BY LEARNING SOMETHING ARTISTIC:

_____

_____

_____

_____

_____

_____

_____

_____

_____

ASSOCIATE WITH PEOPLE WHO ARE LIKELY TO IMPROVE YOU.

Seneca

Someone who improved me today:

_____

_____

_____

If I have seen further it is by standing on the shoulders of giants.

Isaac Newton

The giants who helped me see further today:

_____

_____

_____

God give us the serenity
to accept that
which cannot be changed;
Give us the courage
to change what
should be changed;
Give us the wisdom
to distinguish
one from the other.

Reinhold Niebuhr

DATE: __/__/__

TODAY I ACCEPTED THAT THIS CANNOT BE CHANGED:

_____

_____

_____

_____

_____

_____

_____

DATE: __/__/__

TODAY I BEGAN WORKING TO CHANGE THIS:

_____

_____

_____

_____

_____

_____

I'm not overweight, I am just nine inches too short.

Shelley Winters

I am not _____, I am just _____.

_____

_____

_____

We turn not older with years, but newer every day.

Emily Dickinson

How I turned newer today:

_____

_____

_____

BREATHE IN AND breathe OUT BREATHE IN AND breathe OUT

While sitting, place one hand just below your navel and breathe in slowly through your nose.

Pause for three seconds and breathe out through pursed lips.

Pause for three seconds.

Continue this deep breathing for one minute, feeling your belly rise and fall.

I now feel:

_____

_____

_____

_____

_____

BREATHE IN AND breathe OUT BREATHE IN AND breathe OUT

'Tis the breathing time of day with me.

William Shakespeare

My breathing time of day:

THE BIRD A NEST, THE SPIDER A WEB, MAN FRIENDSHIP.

William Blake

The people who are my nest:

Of all the things that wisdom provides to help one live one's entire life in happiness, the greatest by far is the possession of friendship.

Epicurus

How a friend helped me to live my life in happiness today:

_____

_____

_____

DATE: __/__/__

WHAT MATTERS IN MY LOVE LIFE:

_____

_____

_____

_____

_____

_____

_____

DATE: __/__/__

WHAT MATTERS IN MY WORK LIFE:

_____

_____

_____

_____

_____

_____

_____

All that matters is love and work.

Sigmund Freud

PLACES THAT CENTER ME

A BIT

MORE

EVEN MORE

COMPLETELY

_____

I will arise and go now,
   and go to Innisfree,
And a small cabin build there,
   of clay and wattles made;
Nine bean-rows will I have there,
   a hive for the honey-bee,
And live alone in the bee-loud glade.

William Butler Yeats

A description or drawing of my Innisfree:

Progress is impossible without change, and those who cannot change their minds cannot change anything.

George Bernard Shaw, attrib.

How I changed my mind today:

_____

_____

My progress:

_____

_____

Everything flows and nothing stays.... You cannot step twice into the same river.

Heraclitus

How my river was different today:

_____

_____

_____

EVERY
moment
HAD ITS
pleasure
anD ITS
HOPE.

Jane Austen

DATE: __/__/__

TODAY'S PLEASURE:

_____

_____

_____

_____

_____

_____

_____

DATE: __/__/__

TODAY'S HOPE:

_____

_____

_____

_____

_____

_____

_____

It is our choices, Harry, that show what we truly are, far more than our abilities.

J. K. Rowling

What today's choice shows about me:

_____

_____

_____

THE DIFFICULTY IN LIFE IS THE CHOICE.

George Moore

The difficult choice I made today:

_____

_____

_____

DATE: __/__/__

MY LEARNING GOAL
and how I will get there

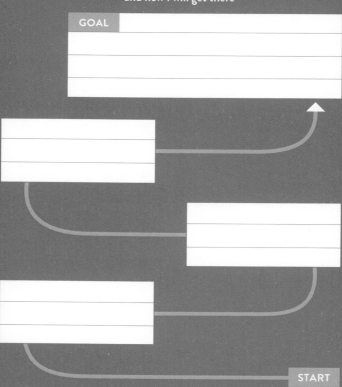

GOAL

START

A small daily task, if it be really daily, will beat the labours of a spasmodic Hercules.

Anthony Trollope

My daily task, beginning today:

_____

_____

How I will make it really daily:

_____

_____

Those who bring sunshine to the lives of others cannot keep it from themselves.

James M. Barrie

Sunshine I brought to the life of another today:

_____

_____

How that brought sunshine to me:

_____

_____

THEY GAVE IT ME— FOR AN UN—BIRTHDAY PRESENT.

Lewis Carroll

An un-birthday present I gave or received today:

_____

_____

_____

DATE: __/__/__

MY ONE PROFOUND INTEREST:

_____

_____

_____

_____

_____

DATE: __/__/__

MY THOUSAND (OR SO) OTHER INTERESTS:

_____

_____

_____

_____

_____

_____

_____

_____

The whole secret of life is to be interested in one thing profoundly and in a thousand things well.

Horace Walpole

THE MOST POWERFUL WEAPON ON EARTH IS THE HUMAN SOUL ON FIRE.

Ferdinand Foch

What fires my soul:

_____

How I used it as a weapon today:

_____

_____

DATE: __/__/__

IF a man HaS noT DISCOVeReD SomeTHING THaT He WILL DIe FOR, He ISN'T FIT TO LIVe.

Martin Luther King, Jr.

What I would die for:

_____

_____

_____

DATE: _/_/_

NO DUTY IS MORE URGENT THAN THAT OF RETURNING THANKS.

Saint Ambrose

How I returned thanks today:

_____

_____

_____

DATE: __/__/__

to: _____
_____
_____

Thank You!

for

_____
_____
_____
_____
_____
_____

Learn as if you were to live forever.

Mahatma Gandhi

A new course of learning I began today:

_____

_____

_____

DATE: _/_/_

SWALLOW ALL YOUR LEARNING IN THE MORNING, BUT DIGEST IT IN COMPANY IN THE EVENINGS.

Lord Chesterfield

Learning I swallowed today:

_____

_____

Company with whom I digested it:

_____

_____

You have to be able to center yourself, to let all of your emotions go.... Don't ever forget that you play with your soul as well as your body.

Kareem Abdul-Jabbar

DATE: __/__/__

HOW I CENTERED MY SOUL TODAY:

_____

_____

_____

_____

_____

_____

_____

DATE: __/__/__

HOW I CENTERED MY BODY TODAY:

_____

_____

_____

_____

_____

_____

_____

No pessimist ever discovered the secrets of the stars, or sailed to an uncharted land, or opened a new heaven to the human spirit.

Helen Keller

My act of optimism today:

_____

_____

_____

The hope of a skinny kid with a funny name who believes that America has a place for him, too.
The audacity of hope!

Barack Obama

My audacious hope:

_____

_____

_____

DATE: __/__/__

TURN OFF / IGNORE / HIDE ALL ELECTRONIC DEVICES FOR *ONE HOUR*.

How I spent my time unplugged:

_____

_____

_____

_____

_____

_____

_____

_____

_____

DATE: __/__/__

Man cannot live by technology alone.

Arnold J. Toynbee

Top Five Electronics I Used Today

_____

_____

_____

_____

_____

Top Five Apps I Opened Today

_____

_____

_____

_____

_____

What else I needed to live today:

_____

_____

PEOPLE WHO CENTER ME

A BIT

MORE

EVEN MORE

COMPLETELY

_____

WE ALL NEED PEOPLE WHO WILL GIVE US FEEDBACK. THAT'S HOW WE IMPROVE.

Bill Gates

Feedback that improved me today:

_____

_____

_____

DATE: __/__/__

WHERE MY TALENT DEVELOPED TODAY:

_____

_____

_____

_____

_____

_____

_____

DATE: __/__/__

WHERE MY CHARACTER DEVELOPED TODAY:

_____

_____

_____

_____

_____

_____

_____

TALENT
DEVELOPS IN
QUIET PLACES,
CHARACTER
IN THE
FULL CURRENT
OF HUMAN
LIFE.

Johann Wolfgang von Goethe

COLORING FREES ME

FLOW WITH WHATEVER MAY HAPPEN AND LET YOUR MIND BE FREE. STAY CENTERED BY ACCEPTING WHATEVER YOU ARE DOING.

Chuang Tzu

How I went with the flow today:

_____

_____

_____

If you want others to be happy, practice compassion. If you want to be happy, practice compassion.

Dalai Lama

How I practiced compassion today:

_____

_____

_____

The man who dies ... rich dies disgraced.

Andrew Carnegie

My gift of money or time today:

_____

_____

_____

DATE: __/__/__

AN UNWANTED DUTY I DID FOR THE FIRST TIME TODAY:

_____

_____

_____

HOW I FELT AFTERWARD:

_____

_____

DATE: __/__/__

AN UNWANTED DUTY I DID TODAY THAT HAS BECOME A HABIT:

_____

_____

_____

HOW I FELT AFTERWARD:

_____

_____

Make it a point
to do something
every day that you
don't want to do.
This is the golden rule
for acquiring the
habit of doing your
duty without pain.

Mark Twain

I believe that if one always looks at the skies, one would end up with wings.

Gustave Flaubert

What skies I looked at today:

_____

_____

_____

Your attitude determines your altitude.

Proverb

My attitude today:

_____

_____

_____

The altitude I reached:

_____

_____

_____

STOP
AND SMELL
THE ROSES

The simple pleasures of the morning:

_____

_____

_____

_____

_____

_____

DATE: __/__/__

When you rise in the morning, form a resolution to make the day a happy one to a fellow-creature.

Sydney Smith

How I resolved to make a fellow-creature happy today:

_____

_____

_____

DATE: __/__/__

Wherever you are—
if you are following
your bliss, you are
enjoying that refreshment,
that life within you,
all the time.

Joseph Campbell

How I followed my bliss today:

_____

_____

_____

DATE: __/__/__

DO WHAT YOU LOVE AND LOVE WHAT YOU DO, AND EVERYTHING ELSE IS DETAIL.

Martina Navratilova

What I love to do:

_____

_____

_____

As you grow older,
you will discover
that you have two hands,
one for helping
yourself, the other for
helping others.

Audrey Hepburn

DATE: ___/___/___

HOW I HELPED MYSELF TODAY:

_____

_____

_____

_____

_____

_____

_____

DATE: ___/___/___

HOW I HELPED OTHERS TODAY:

_____

_____

_____

_____

_____

_____

_____

Resolve to edge in a little reading every day, if it is but a single sentence. If you gain fifteen minutes a day, it will make itself felt at the end of the year.

Horace Mann

What I read today:

_____

_____

_____

Beware you be not swallowed up in books! An ounce of love is worth a pound of knowledge.

John Wesley

How I balanced my learning with loving today:

_____

_____

_____

S-T-R-E-T-C-H

STRETCH YOUR NECK TO RELAX

Bend your head forward and slightly to the right.

With your right hand, gently pull your head downward. You'll feel a nice, easy stretch along the back left side of your neck.

Hold for about thirty seconds.

Repeat on the opposite side.

HOW I FEEL NOW:

_____

_____

_____

_____

_____

STRETCH YOUR SHOULDERS TO RELEASE TENSION

Bring your left arm across your body and hold it with your right arm, either above or below the elbow.

Hold for about thirty seconds.

Switch arms and repeat.

HOW I FEEL NOW:

_____

_____

_____

_____

_____

NOTHING GREAT WAS EVER ACHIEVED WITHOUT ENTHUSIASM.

Ralph Waldo Emerson

What I am enthusiastic about today:

_____

_____

_____

ANYTHING THAT I DO I PURSUE 110 PERCENT.

Apolo Anton Ohno

What I pursued 110 percent today:

_____

_____

_____

DATE: __/__/__

CHAOS I ADORED TODAY:

_____

_____

_____

_____

_____

_____

_____

DATE: __/__/__

ORDER I PRODUCED TODAY:

_____

_____

_____

_____

_____

_____

_____

WE ADORE
CHAOS
BECAUSE
WE LOVE
TO PRODUCE
ORDER.

M. C. Escher

Minds are like parachutes. They only function when they are open.

James Dewar, attrib.

How I opened my mind today:

_____

_____

_____

The mind, once expanded to the dimensions of larger ideas, never returns to its original size.

Oliver Wendell Holmes

A large idea that expanded my mind today:

_____

_____

_____

DATE: __/__/__

While sitting, take several slow, deep breaths in and out.

As you breathe in, say quietly, "I am"; as you breathe out, say quietly, "at peace."

Repeat two or three times.

I now feel:

_____

_____

_____

_____

_____

_____

The quieter you become, the more you can hear.

Ram Dass

What I heard in the quiet today:

_____

_____

_____

THE LESS ROUTINE THE MORE OF LIFE.

Amos Bronson Alcott

How I broke loose from routine today:

_____

_____

_____

DATE: __/__/__

ROUTINE IS LIBERATING. IT MAKES YOU FEEL IN CONTROL.

Carol Shields

How today's routine made me feel in control:

_____

_____

_____

DATE: __/__/__

WHAT I HAVE AND REJOICED FOR TODAY:

DATE: __/__/__

WHAT I DON'T HAVE AND DID NOT GRIEVE FOR TODAY:

He is a wise man
who does not
grieve for
the things which
he has not,
but rejoices
for those which
he has.

Epictetus

FOOD THAT CENTERS ME

A BIT

MORE

EVEN MORE

COMPLETELY

_____

And as soon as I had recognized
the taste of the piece of madeleine
dipped in lime-blossom tea
that my aunt used to give me . . .
immediately the old gray house
on the street, where her bedroom was,
came like a stage set . . . and all
of Combray and its surroundings.

Marcel Proust

My "madeleine" experience today:

_____

_____

_____

THE MIND IS NOT A VESSEL TO BE FILLED BUT A FIRE TO BE KINDLED.

Plutarch

How I kindled my mind today:

_____

_____

_____

The mind can also be an erogenous zone.

Raquel Welch

What turned my mind on today:

_____

_____

_____

A PROPENSITY TO HOPE AND JOY IS REAL RICHES.

David Hume

DATE: __/__/__

WHAT I HOPED FOR TODAY:

_____

_____

_____

_____

_____

_____

DATE: __/__/__

WHAT GAVE ME JOY TODAY:

_____

_____

_____

_____

_____

_____

DATE: ___/___/___

A STRONG BODY MAKES THE MIND STRONG.

Thomas Jefferson

How I strengthened my body today:

_____

_____

How this strengthened my mind:

_____

_____

Every man is the builder of a temple, called his body.

Henry David Thoreau

How I cared for my temple today:

_____

_____

_____

MY COMMUNITY GOAL
and how I will get there

GOAL

START

No man is an island,
Entire of itself,
Every man is a piece of
  the continent,
A part of the main.

John Donne

My continent:

_____

_____

_____

The world is a looking-glass, and gives back to every man the reflection of his own face. Frown at it, and it will in turn look sourly upon you; laugh at it and with it, and it is a jolly, kind companion.

William Makepeace Thackeray

How I want the world to reflect me:

_____

_____

_____

HAPPINESS IS A HOW; NOT A WHAT. A TALENT, NOT AN OBJECT.

Hermann Hesse

How I made myself happy today:

_____

_____

_____

DATE: __/__/__

A KINDNESS SHOWN TO ME TODAY:

_____

_____

_____

_____

_____

_____

_____

DATE: __/__/__

A KINDNESS I PASSED ON TODAY:

_____

_____

_____

_____

_____

_____

_____

Have you had a
kindness shown?
Pass it on;
'Twas not given
for thee alone;
Pass it on.

Henry Burton

Not being beautiful ... forced me to develop my inner resources. The pretty girl has a handicap to overcome.

Golda Meir

My handicap:

_____

_____

My inner resources:

_____

_____

When I was around eighteen, I looked in the mirror and said, "You're either going to love yourself or hate yourself." And I decided to love myself.

Queen Latifah

What I decided to love about myself today:

_____

_____

_____

DATE: __/__/__

to: _____
_____

Thank You!

for

_____
_____
_____
_____
_____
_____

My gift is my song and this one's for you.

Elton John

My gift is my:

_____

_____

_____

Today I gave this gift to:

_____

_____

_____

IT IS NOT ENOUGH TO HAVE A GOOD MIND; THE MAIN THING IS TO USE IT WELL.

René Descartes

How I used my mind well today:

_____

_____

_____

NATURAL ABILITIES ARE LIKE NATURAL PLANTS, THAT NEED PRUNING BY STUDY.

Francis Bacon

My natural abilities:

_____

_____

How I pruned them today:

_____

_____

The two kinds of
people on earth
I mean,
Are the people
who lift
and the people
who lean.

Ella Wheeler Wilcox

DATE: __/__/__

HOW I LET OTHERS LEAN ON ME TODAY:

_____

_____

_____

_____

_____

_____

_____

DATE: __/__/__

HOW I LEANED ON OTHERS TODAY:

_____

_____

_____

_____

_____

_____

_____

Yes, there is a Nirvanah;
it is in leading your
sheep to a green
pasture, and in putting
your child to sleep,
and in writing the last
line of your poem.

Kahlil Gibran

My Nirvanah today:

_____

_____

_____

The least of things with a meaning is worth more in life than the greatest of things without it.

Carl Gustav Jung

A small thing with meaning today:

_____

_____

_____

DATE: _/_/_

THE THING WITH HIGH-TECH IS THAT YOU ALWAYS END UP USING SCISSORS.

David Hockney

The low-tech device I fell back on today:

_____

_____

_____

unplug

TURN OFF / IGNORE / HIDE ALL ELECTRONIC DEVICES FOR *TWO HOURS*.

How I spent my time unplugged:

_____

_____

_____

_____

_____

_____

_____

_____

LITERATURE THAT CENTERS ME

A BIT

MORE

EVEN MORE

COMPLETELY

_____

Reading is to the mind what exercise is to the body.

Richard Steele

How I exercised my mind today:

_____

_____

_____

DATE: __/__/__

MY IMPOSSIBLE DREAM:

_____

_____

_____

_____

_____

_____

DATE: __/__/__

HOW MY IMPOSSIBLE DREAM BECAME INEVITABLE:

_____

_____

_____

_____

_____

_____

So many of our dreams at first seem impossible, then they seem improbable, and then, when we summon the will, they soon become inevitable.

Christopher Reeve

Come, let us give a little time to folly… and even in a melancholy day let us find time for an hour of pleasure.

Saint Bonaventura

A little time I gave to folly today:

_____

_____

_____

DATE: ___/___/___

COLORING BRINGS ME PLEASURE

DATE: __/__/__

All men by nature desire knowledge.

Aristotle

What I wanted to learn today:

_____

_____

_____

IMAGINATION IS MORE IMPORTANT THAN KNOWLEDGE.

Albert Einstein

What I imagined today:

_____

_____

_____

The grand Perhaps!

Robert Browning

DATE: __/__/__

PERHAPS TODAY:

_____

_____

_____

_____

_____

_____

_____

DATE: __/__/__

PERHAPS TOMORROW:

_____

_____

_____

_____

_____

_____

_____

ALMOST ANY MAN MAY LIKE THE SPIDER SPIN FROM HIS OWN INWARDS HIS OWN AIRY CITADEL.

John Keats

The airy Citadel spun from inside me today:

_____

_____

_____

This is the Thing that I was born to do.

Samuel Daniel

The Thing I did today:

_____

_____

_____

The simple things that bring me pleasure as I work:

_____

_____

_____

_____

_____

_____

BLESSED IS HE WHO HAS FOUND HIS WORK.

Thomas Carlyle

Work that made me feel blessed today:

_____

_____

_____

There is no exercise better for the heart than reaching down and lifting people up.

John Andrew Holmes

Someone I lifted up today:

_____

How that made my heart feel:

_____

_____

Sometimes you have to step outside of the person you've been and remember the person you were meant to be. The person you want to be. The person you are.

H. G. Wells

The person I am meant to be:

_____

The person I want to be:

_____

The person I am:

_____

DATE: __/__/__

HOW I CHANGED TODAY:

_____

_____

_____

_____

_____

_____

_____

DATE: __/__/__

WHAT I HELD FAST TO TODAY:

_____

_____

_____

_____

_____

_____

_____

A capacity
to change
is indispensable.
Equally
indispensable is
the capacity
to hold fast to that
which is good.

John Foster Dulles

Go far; come near;
You still must be
The center of your own
small mystery.

Walter de la Mare

Where I found my own small mystery:

_____

_____

_____

You can tell a lot about a fellow's character by his way of eating jelly beans.

Ronald Reagan

What I do that reveals my character:

_____

_____

_____

S-T-R-E-T-C-H

I STRETCHED MY HEART BY SAYING THESE KIND WORDS TODAY:

_____

_____

_____

_____

_____

_____

_____

_____

DATE: __/__/__

YOUR H-E-A-R-T

I STRETCHED MY HEART BY DOING THIS KIND DEED TODAY:

_____

_____

_____

_____

_____

_____

_____

_____

Learn to live, and live to learn, Ignorance like a fire doth burn, Little tasks make large return.

Bayard Taylor

My little tasks today:

_____

_____

My large return:

_____

_____

I now want to
know all things
under the sun, and
the moon, too....
Knowledge is
life with wings.

Kahlil Gibran

What gave me wings today:

_____

_____

_____

We have
no more right
to consume
happiness without
producing it
than to consume
wealth without
producing it.

George Bernard Shaw

DATE: __/__/__

HAPPINESS I CONSUMED TODAY:

_____

_____

_____

_____

_____

_____

DATE: __/__/__

HAPPINESS I PRODUCED TODAY:

_____

_____

_____

_____

_____

_____

The kind of beauty I want most is the hard-to-get kind that comes from within—strength, courage, dignity.

Ruby Dee

My beauty rated on a scale of 1 to 10:

Strength _____

Courage _____

Dignity _____

OUR DEEDS DETERMINE US, AS MUCH AS WE DETERMINE OUR DEEDS.

George Eliot

A deed that determined me today:

_____

_____

_____

BREATHE IN AND BREATHE OUT BREATHE IN AND BREATHE OUT

Sit comfortably with your eyes closed.

Breathe deeply for a few minutes, in through your nose and out through pursed lips.

Picture yourself in a beautiful place you know.

What do you smell? What do you hear? What do you feel? What do you taste?

Focus on your senses, and continue for ten minutes.

My beautiful place:

_____

I now feel:

_____

_____

_____

BREATHE IN AND BREATHE OUT BREATHE IN AND BREATHE OUT

Is it so small a thing
To have enjoy'd the sun,
To have lived light
        in the spring,
To have loved, to have
        thought, to have done?

Matthew Arnold

What small thing I:

[   ] enjoyed _____

[   ] lived _____

[   ] loved _____

[   ] thought _____

[   ] did _____

Experience is not what happens to a man; it is what a man does with what happens to him.

Aldous Huxley

An experience I had today:

_____

_____

What I will do with it:

_____

_____

DATE: __/__/__

RESOLVE TO PERFORM WHAT YOU OUGHT. PERFORM WITHOUT FAIL WHAT YOU RESOLVE.

Benjamin Franklin

What I ought to do:

_____

_____

_____

_____

[ ] Did it.

DATE: __/__/__

A THOUGHT TODAY THAT TRANSFORMED ME:

_____

_____

_____

_____

_____

_____

DATE: __/__/__

A POSSIBILITY TODAY THAT TRANSFORMED ME:

_____

_____

_____

_____

_____

_____

A thought,
even a possibility,
can shatter us
and transform us.

Friedrich Wilhelm Nietzsche

ART THAT CENTERS ME

A BIT

MORE

EVEN MORE

COMPLETELY

_____

ART HAS SOMETHING TO DO WITH THE ACHIEVEMENT OF STILLNESS IN THE MIDST OF CHAOS.

Saul Bellow

Art that stilled me today:

_____

_____

_____

Whatever you are is never enough; you must find a way to accept something however small from the other to make you whole.

Chinua Achebe

What I accepted from another today to make me whole:

_____

_____

_____

TO LOSE BALANCE SOMETIMES FOR LOVE IS PART OF LIVING a BALANCED LIFE.

Elizabeth Gilbert

How love unbalanced me today:

_____

_____

How that helped to balance my life:

_____

_____

A good head and a good heart are always a formidable combination.

Nelson Mandela

DATE: __/__/__

HOW MY GOOD HEAD LED ME TO ACT FORMIDABLY TODAY:

_____

_____

_____

_____

_____

_____

DATE: __/__/__

HOW MY GOOD HEART LED ME TO ACT FORMIDABLY TODAY:

_____

_____

_____

_____

_____

_____

He can't think without his hat.

Samuel Beckett

What I can't think without:

_____

_____

_____

GO TO THE PINE IF YOU WANT TO LEARN ABOUT THE PINE.

Matsuo Bashō

What I want to learn about today:

_____

_____

How I will do it:

_____

_____

_____

DATE: __/__/__

MY HEALTH GOAL
and how I will get there

GOAL	

START

FOR THE MAN SOUND IN BODY AND SERENE IN MIND THERE IS NO SUCH THING AS BAD WEATHER!

George Gissing

How my sound body and serene mind defied bad weather today:

_____

_____

_____

Great thoughts come from the heart.

Luc de Clapiers, Marquis de Vauvenargues

How my heart led me to an insight today:

_____

_____

_____

We are lonesome animals. We spend all our life trying to be less lonesome.

John Steinbeck

How I became less lonesome today:

_____

_____

_____

The right attitude
can transform a barrier
into a blessing,
an obstacle
into an opportunity,
or a stumbling block
into a stepping-stone.

Cory Booker

DATE: __/__/__

A BARRIER THAT BECAME A BLESSING TODAY:

_____

_____

_____

DATE: __/__/__

AN OBSTACLE THAT BECAME AN OPPORTUNITY TODAY:

_____

_____

_____

DATE: __/__/__

A STUMBLING BLOCK THAT BECAME A STEPPING-STONE TODAY:

_____

_____

_____

There is only one success— to be able to spend your life in your own way.

Christopher Morley

How I spent today in my own way:

_____

_____

_____

DATE: __/__/__

WE MUST BE THE CHANGE WE WISH TO SEE IN THE WORLD.

Mahatma Gandhi

The change I wish to see in the world:

_____

_____

How I can contribute to this:

_____

_____

A bit of fragrance always clings to the hand that gives you roses.

Chinese Proverb

Today I gave roses to:

_____

_____

The fragrance clinging to my hand:

_____

_____

DATE: ___/___/___

to: _____

_____

_____

Thank You!

for

_____

_____

_____

_____

_____

_____

_____

LIFE IS A BLANK CANVAS, AND YOU NEED TO THROW ALL THE PAINT ON IT YOU CAN.

Danny Kaye

Paint I threw on life's blank canvas today:

_____

_____

_____

DATE: __/__/__

Do things; be sane; don't fritter away your time; create, act, take a place wherever you are and be somebody: get action.

Theodore Roosevelt

An action I took today:

_____

_____

_____

DATE: __/__/__

THE ANSWERS I LEARNED TODAY:

_____

_____

_____

_____

_____

_____

_____

DATE: __/__/__

THE QUESTION I ASKED TODAY:

_____

_____

_____

_____

_____

_____

We have learned
the answers,
all the answers:
It is the question
that we
do not know.

Archibald MacLeish

Each morning sees
   some task begin,
Each evening sees it close;
Something attempted,
   something done,
Has earned a night's repose.

Henry Wadsworth Longfellow

What I did today to earn a night's repose:

_____

_____

_____

To every thing there is a season,

and a time to every purpose

under the heaven:

A time to be born, and a time to die...

A time to weep, and a time to laugh;

a time to mourn, and a time to dance.

Ecclesiastes

Today is a time to:

_____

_____

_____

DATE: __/__/__

TURN OFF / IGNORE / HIDE ALL ELECTRONIC DEVICES
FOR *THREE HOURS.*

How I spent my time unplugged:

_____

_____

_____

_____

_____

_____

_____

_____

_____

DATE: __/__/__

ALMOST EVERYTHING WILL WORK AGAIN IF YOU UNPLUG IT FOR A FEW MINUTES, INCLUDING YOU.

Anne Lamott

What began to work again when I unplugged:

_____

_____

_____

Perfume is the most intense form of memory.

Jean-Paul Guerlain

An intensely fragrant memory today:

_____

_____

_____

SMELLS THAT CENTER ME

A BIT

MORE

EVEN MORE

COMPLETELY

_____

SELF-KNOWLEDGE IS THE BEGINNING OF SELF-IMPROVEMENT.

Baltasar Gracián

DATE: __/__/__

WHAT I LEARNED ABOUT MYSELF TODAY:

DATE: __/__/__

HOW SELF-KNOWLEDGE IMPROVED ME TODAY:

DATE: ___/___/___

The main thing to do is relax and let your talent do the work.

Charles Barkley

How I relaxed today:

_____

_____

How my talent worked:

_____

_____

Happiness is good health and a bad memory.

Ingrid Bergman

What I am glad to have forgotten:

_____

_____

_____

What a wonderful life I've had! I only wish I'd realized it sooner.

Colette

What makes my life wonderful:

_____

_____

_____

DATE: __/__/__

RELATIONS I AM GLAD FATE CHOSE FOR ME:

_____

_____

_____

_____

_____

_____

_____

DATE: __/__/__

FRIENDS I AM GLAD I CHOSE:

_____

_____

_____

_____

_____

_____

_____

FATE CHOOSES YOUR RELATIONS, YOU CHOOSE YOUR FRIENDS.

Jacques Delille

Take time every day to do something silly.

Philipa Walker

Something silly I did today:

_____

_____

_____

ALL INTELLECTUAL IMPROVEMENT ARISES FROM LEISURE.

Samuel Johnson

How leisure improved my mind today:

_____

_____

_____

STOP
**AND SMELL
THE ROSES**

The simple things at home that bring me pleasure:

_____

_____

_____

_____

_____

_____

Blessed are they who see beautiful things in humble places where other people see nothing.

Camille Pissarro

Something beautiful I saw in a humble place today:

_____

_____

_____

REGARD NOT SO MUCH WHAT THE WORLD THINKS OF THEE, AS WHAT THOU THINKEST OF THYSELF.

Thomas Fuller

What I thought of myself today:

_____

_____

_____

Very early in life I realized that the most important relationship is the one you have with yourself.

Diane von Furstenberg

How I treated myself today:

_____

_____

_____

To attain knowledge, add things every day. To attain wisdom, subtract things every day.

Lao Tzu

DATE: __/__/__

WHAT I ADDED TODAY:

_____

_____

_____

_____

_____

_____

_____

DATE: __/__/__

WHAT I SUBTRACTED TODAY:

_____

_____

_____

_____

_____

_____

_____

INNER SPACE IS THE REAL FRONTIER.

Gloria Steinem

What I found in my inner space today:

_____

_____

_____

Nothing contributes so much to tranquilize the mind as a steady purpose.

Mary Shelley

My steady purpose today:

_____

_____

_____

S-T-R-E-T-C-H

**I STRETCHED MY MIND TODAY
BY LEARNING SOMETHING PRACTICAL:**

_____

_____

_____

_____

_____

_____

_____

_____

DATE: __/__/__

your M-I-N-D

I STRETCHED MY MIND TODAY
BY LEARNING SOMETHING IMPRACTICAL:

_____

_____

_____

_____

_____

_____

_____

_____

_____

Life is not meant to be easy.

John Malcolm Fraser

A challenge I met today:

_____

_____

_____

ALL EXPERIENCE IS AN ARCH, TO BUILD UPON.

Henry Brooks Adams

An experience I built upon today:

_____

_____

_____

DATE: ___/___/___

THE WAY I FOUND TODAY:

_____

_____

_____

_____

_____

_____

_____

DATE: ___/___/___

THE WAY I MADE TODAY:

_____

_____

_____

_____

_____

_____

_____

I WILL
EITHER FIND
A WAY, OR
MAKE ONE.

Hannibal

The only means of strengthening one's intellect is to make up one's mind about nothing—to let the mind be a thoroughfare for all thoughts. Not a selective party.

John Keats

I haven't made up my mind about:

_____

_____

_____

THE REAL QUESTION IS NOT WHERE DO IDEAS COME FROM BUT WHERE DO THEY GO.

Paul Beatty

Today's idea:

_____

_____

Where it went:

_____

_____

DATE: __/__/__

Sitting or standing, count down from 10 to 0
as you breathe deeply, saying the number as you
inhale, then exhaling slowly.

I now feel:

_____

_____

_____

_____

_____

_____

_____

Breathing in, I calm my body. Breathing out, I smile.

Thich Nhat Hanh

How breathing centered me today:

_____

_____

_____

EVEN WHEN THEY TEACH, MEN LEARN.

Seneca the Younger

What I learned by teaching today:

_____

_____

_____

FEW HAVE BEEN TAUGHT TO ANY PURPOSE WHO HAVE NOT BEEN THEIR OWN TEACHERS.

Joshua Reynolds

What I learned on my own today:

_____

_____

_____

It is a good idea
sometimes to
think of the
importance and
dignity of our
everyday duties.

Laura Ingalls Wilder

DATE: __/__/__

THE IMPORTANCE OF MY EVERYDAY DUTIES:

_____

_____

_____

_____

_____

_____

_____

DATE: __/__/__

THE DIGNITY OF MY EVERYDAY DUTIES:

_____

_____

_____

_____

_____

_____

_____

I cannot pretend to feel impartial about the colours. I rejoice with the brilliant ones, and am generally sorry for the poor browns.

Winston Churchill

Colors that made me rejoice today:

_____

_____

_____

COLORS THAT CENTER ME

The clearest way into the Universe is through a forest wilderness.

John Muir

How I entered the Universe through a wilderness today:

_____

_____

_____

All characters,
*   movements, growths—*
*   a few noticed,*
*   myriads unnoticed,*
Through Mannahatta's
*   streets I walking, these*
*   things gathering...*

Walt Whitman

Characters, movements, or growths I gathered on the streets today:

_____

_____

_____

DATE: __/__/__

WHAT I TAUGHT SOMEONE TODAY:

_____

_____

_____

_____

_____

_____

_____

DATE: __/__/__

WHAT I LEARNED TODAY:

_____

_____

_____

_____

_____

_____

_____

It is the province
of knowledge
to speak and it is
the privilege
of wisdom to listen.

Oliver Wendell Holmes

Character is a by-product; it is produced in the great manufacture of daily duty.

Woodrow Wilson

My character-producing duties today:

_____

_____

_____

I am an IDEALIST. I DON'T KNOW WHERE I'M GOING BUT I'M ON THE WAY.

Carl Sandburg

How I am on the way:

_____

_____

_____

DATE: __/__/__

MY RELATIONSHIP GOAL
and how I will get there

GOAL	

START

A friend is a present you give to yourself.

Robert Louis Stevenson

A present I gave to myself today:

_____

_____

_____

Life is not a spectator sport.... If you're going to spend your whole life in the grandstand just watching what goes on, in my opinion, you're wasting your life.

Jackie Robinson

What I did on the field today:

_____

_____

_____

THE SIDELINES ARE NOT WHERE YOU WANT TO LIVE YOUR LIFE. THE WORLD NEEDS YOU IN THE ARENA.

Tim Cook

What I did in the arena today:

_____

_____

_____

Let me be
a little kinder,
Let me be a
little blinder
To the faults
of those
around me.

Edgar A. Guest

DATE: __/__/__

HOW I WAS A LITTLE KINDER TODAY:

_____

_____

_____

_____

_____

_____

DATE: __/__/__

HOW I WAS A LITTLE BLINDER TODAY:

_____

_____

_____

_____

_____

I am in the world to change the world.

Muriel Rukeyser

Why I am in the world:

_____

_____

_____

[THE PASSIONS] ARE THE WINDS THAT FILL THE SHIP'S SAILS. SOMETIMES THEY SUBMERGE THE SHIP, BUT WITHOUT THEM THE SHIP COULD NOT SAIL.

Voltaire

The passions that fill my sails today:

_____

_____

_____

DO GOOD BY STEALTH, AND BLUSH TO FIND IT FAME.

Alexander Pope

A good deed I did by stealth today:

_____

_____

_____

to: _____

_____

_____

Thank You!
for

_____

_____

_____

_____

_____

_____

LEARN WHAT YOU ARE AND BE SUCH.

Pindar

What I learned about myself today:

_____

_____

_____

We are what we pretend to be.

Kurt Vonnegut

What I pretended to be today:

_____

_____

_____

DATE: __/__/__

TODAY'S SUDDEN THOUGHT:

_____

_____

_____

_____

_____

_____

_____

DATE: __/__/__

TODAY'S SPLENDID THOUGHT:

_____

_____

_____

_____

_____

_____

_____

STUNG
BY THE
SPLENDOR
OF A
SUDDEN
THOUGHT.

Robert Browning

DATE: __/__/__

SERVICE IS THE RENT THAT YOU PAY FOR ROOM ON THIS EARTH.

Shirley Chisholm

How I served today:

_____

_____

_____

Do all the good you can,

By all the means you can,

In all the ways you can,

In all the places you can,

At all the times you can,

To all the people you can,

As long as ever you can.

Anonymous

All the good I can do today:

_____

_____

_____

DATE: __/__/__

TURN OFF / IGNORE / HIDE ALL ELTECTRONIC DEVICES
FOR *ONE EVENING.*

How I spent my time unplugged:

_____

_____

_____

_____

_____

_____

_____

_____

_____

Silence is as full of potential wisdom and wit as the unhewn marble of great sculpture.

Aldous Huxley

What I discovered in silence today:

_____

_____

_____

MUSIC THAT CENTERS ME

A BIT

MORE

EVEN MORE

COMPLETELY

_____

MUSIC HAS CHARMS TO SOOTHE A SAVAGE BEAST.

William Congreve

How music soothed me today:

_____

_____

_____

THEY MUST OFTEN CHANGE WHO WOULD BE CONSTANT IN HAPPINESS OR WISDOM.

Confucius

DATE: __/__/__

CHANGE THAT MADE ME HAPPY TODAY:

_____

_____

_____

_____

_____

_____

_____

DATE: __/__/__

CHANGE THAT MADE ME WISE TODAY:

_____

_____

_____

_____

_____

_____

_____

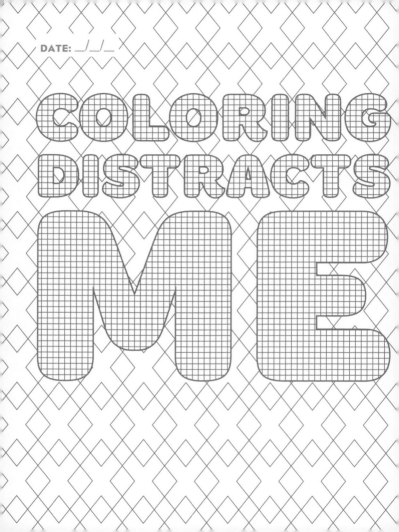

DATE: _/_/_

COLORING DISTRACTS ME

Each person deserves a day
away in which no problems
are confronted,
no solutions searched for.
Each of us needs
to withdraw from the
cares which will
not withdraw from us.

Maya Angelou

How I withdrew from my cares today:

_____

_____

_____

WISDOM IS NOT THE PURCHASE OF A DAY.

Thomas Paine

It took me_____years_____months_____days,

to become wise about:

_____

_____

_____

They know enough who know how to learn.

Henry Adams

What I want to know today:

_____

_____

How I will learn it:

_____

_____

THE GOOD
LIFE IS ONE
INSPIRED BY
LOVE AND
GUIDED BY
KNOWLEDGE.

Bertrand Russell

DATE: __/__/__

LOVE THAT INSPIRED ME TODAY:

_____

_____

_____

_____

_____

_____

_____

DATE: __/__/__

KNOWLEDGE THAT GUIDED ME TODAY:

_____

_____

_____

_____

_____

_____

_____

One way to open your eyes
to unnoticed beauty is to ask
yourself, "What if I had never
seen this before? What if I knew
I would never see it again?"

Rachel Carson

My favorite sight:

_____

_____

What if I had never seen this before?

_____

_____

What if I knew I would never see this again?

_____

_____

The poetry of earth is never dead.

John Keats

Earth's poem for me today:

_____

_____

_____

STOP
AND SMELL
THE ROSES

The simple things that bring me pleasure in the evening:

_____

_____

_____

_____

_____

_____

Evening, you bring back
all that bright dawn scattered.
You bring a sheep, you
bring a goat, you bring a
child back to its mother.

Sappho

What this evening brought back to me:

_____

_____

_____

True happiness... is not attained through self-gratification, but through fidelity to a worthy purpose.

Helen Keller

My worthy purpose:

_____

_____

_____

Happiness is when what you think, what you say, and what you do are in harmony.

Mahatma Gandhi

What I thought today:

_____

_____

What I said today:

_____

_____

What I did today:

_____

_____

To look up
and not down,
To look forward
and not back,
To look out
and not in, and
To lend a hand.

Edward Everett Hale

DATE: __/__/__

HOW I LOOKED:

[ ] UP _____

_____

[ ] FORWARD _____

_____

[ ] OUT _____

_____

DATE: __/__/__

HOW I LENT A HAND TODAY:

_____

_____

_____

_____

_____

_____

_____

A FRIEND IS ONE WHO KNOWS YOU AND LOVES YOU JUST THE SAME.

Elbert Hubbard

My unconditional friend:

_____

_____

_____

[Friendship] redoubleth joys, and cutteth griefs in halves.

Francis Bacon

How friendship redoubled my joys or halved my griefs today:

_____

_____

_____

S-T-R-E-T-C-H

STRETCH YOUR QUADRICEPS TO REDUCE STRESS

Stand near a wall or a piece of sturdy exercise equipment for support.

Grasp your ankle and gently pull your heel up and back until you feel a stretch in the front of your thigh.

Tighten your stomach muscles to prevent your stomach from sagging outward, and keep your knees close together.

Hold for about thirty seconds.

Switch legs and repeat.

HOW I FEEL NOW:

_____

_____

_____

YOUR B-O-D-Y

STRETCH YOUR CALVES TO UNTIGHTEN

Stand at arm's length from a wall or a piece of sturdy exercise equipment.

Place your right foot behind your left foot.

Slowly bend your left leg forward, keeping your right knee straight and your right heel on the floor.

Hold your back straight and your hips forward. Don't rotate your feet inward or outward.

Hold for about thirty seconds.

Switch legs and repeat.

HOW I FEEL NOW:

_____

_____

_____

TO BE CONSCIOUS OF ONE'S IGNORANCE IS THE BEGINNING OF WISDOM.

N. Sri Ram

What I realized I didn't know today:

_____

_____

_____

WISDOM HEARS ONE THING AND UNDERSTANDS THREE THINGS.

Chinese proverb

What I heard today:

_____

What I understood:

1) _____

2) _____

3) _____

Life is short ...
O, be swift to
love! Make haste
to be kind.

Henri-Frédéric Amiel

DATE: __/__/__

HOW I LOVED TODAY:

_____

_____

_____

_____

_____

_____

_____

DATE: __/__/__

HOW I WAS KIND TODAY:

_____

_____

_____

_____

_____

_____

I was brought up to believe that how I saw myself was more important than how others saw me.

Anwar el-Sadat

How I see myself today:

_____

_____

_____

NO one can make you feel inferior without your consent.

Eleanor Roosevelt

How I refused to feel inferior today:

_____

_____

_____

DATE: __/__/__

Stroll outdoors with no purpose or direction for at least ten minutes.

Relax, take short steps, smile, and open yourself. Experience your body's movement, breathing in and out to its rhythm.

Allow sad thoughts and worries to slip away as you walk.

I now feel:

_____

_____

_____

_____

_____

I am a slow walker, but I never walk back.

Abraham Lincoln

How I walked today:

_____

_____

_____

We are made of star-stuff.

Carl Sagan

My star-stuff:

_____

_____

_____

Trust to that prompting within you.

Ralph Waldo Emerson

A prompting within me today:

_____

_____

_____

You make a
difference every
single day.
And you get to
choose what sort
of difference you
want to make.

Jane Goodall

DATE: __/__/__

A DIFFERENCE I MADE TO A PERSON TODAY:

_____

_____

_____

_____

_____

_____

_____

DATE: __/__/__

A DIFFERENCE I MADE IN THE WORLD TODAY:

_____

_____

_____

_____

_____

_____

_____

Things won are done; joy's soul lies in the doing.

William Shakespeare

What I did today that brought me joy:

_____

_____

_____

ACTIVITIES THAT CENTER ME

A BIT

MORE

EVEN MORE

COMPLETELY

_____

AS A FIELD, HOWEVER FERTILE, CANNOT BE FRUITFUL WITHOUT CULTIVATION, NEITHER CAN A MIND WITHOUT LEARNING.

Cicero

How I cultivated my mind today:

_____

_____

_____

WHEN PEOPLE WILL NOT WEED THEIR OWN MINDS, THEY ARE APT TO BE OVERRUN WITH NETTLES.

Horace Walpole

Nettles I weeded out of my mind today:

_____

_____

_____

DATE: __/__/__

A WARM WORD OF KINDNESS I SPOKE TODAY:

_____

_____

_____

_____

_____

_____

_____

DATE: __/__/__

A WARM WORD OF KINDNESS I RECEIVED TODAY:

_____

_____

_____

_____

_____

_____

one kind
word can
warm
three
winter
months.

Japanese proverb

STAY OPEN, FOREVER, SO OPEN IT HURTS, AND THEN OPEN UP SOME MORE.

George Saunders

Today I opened myself up in this way:

_____

_____

_____

The door that nobody else will go in at, seems always to swing open widely for me.

Clara Barton

The door that swung open for me today:

_____

_____

What happened when I went through:

_____

_____

DATE: __/__/__

MY CREATIVE GOAL
and how I will get there

GOAL

START

A genius! For thirty-seven years I've practiced fourteen hours a day, and now they call me a genius!

Pablo de Sarasate

How I am practicing to become a genius:

_____

_____

_____

The highest wisdom is continual cheerfulness; such a state, like the region above the moon, is always clear and serene.

Michel de Montaigne

What made me cheerful today:

_____

_____

_____

It is better to be high-spirited, even though one makes more mistakes, than to be narrow-minded and all too prudent.

Vincent van Gogh

How I acted on my high spirits today:

_____

Any mistakes?

_____

Knowledge from books; wisdom from life.

Jewish proverb

DATE: __/__/__

KNOWLEDGE I LEARNED FROM BOOKS TODAY:

_____

_____

_____

_____

_____

_____

_____

DATE: __/__/__

WISDOM I LEARNED FROM LIFE TODAY:

_____

_____

_____

_____

_____

_____

_____

OUR GREATEST GLORY IS NOT IN NEVER FALLING, BUT IN RISING EVERY TIME WE FALL.

Confucius

Today's fall:

_____

_____

How I rose:

_____

_____

I can accept failure, everyone fails at something. But I can't accept not trying.

Michael Jordan

What I failed at today:

_____

_____

How I tried again:

_____

_____

BEHOLD, I DO NOT GIVE LECTURES OR A LITTLE CHARITY, WHEN I GIVE I GIVE MYSELF.

Walt Whitman

What I gave of myself today:

_____

_____

_____

DATE: __/__/__

to: _____
_____
_____

Thank You!

for

_____
_____
_____
_____
_____
_____

JOY IS NOT IN THINGS; IT IS IN US.

Richard Wagner

The joy in me today:

_____

_____

_____

THERE IS NO JOY BUT CALM!

Alfred, Lord Tennyson

The joyful calm in me today:

_____

_____

_____

DATE: __/__/__

A BATTLE I'M GLAD I AVOIDED AT WORK OR SCHOOL TODAY:

_____

_____

_____

_____

_____

_____

_____

DATE: __/__/__

A BATTLE I'M GLAD I AVOIDED AT HOME TODAY:

_____

_____

_____

_____

_____

_____

Part of the
happiness of
life consists
not in
fighting battles,
but in
avoiding them.

Norman Vincent Peale

Before you speak, let your words
pass through three gates.
At the first gate ask yourself,
"Is it true?" At the second
ask, "Is it necessary?"
At the third gate ask, "Is it kind?"

Sufi saying

What I said today that was true, necessary, and kind:

_____

_____

_____

To love and be loved—this on earth is the highest bliss.

Heinrich Heine

Whom I love:

_____

_____

_____

Who loves me:

_____

_____

_____

DATE: __/__/__

TURN OFF / IGNORE / HIDE ALL ELECTRONIC DEVICES FOR *A FULL DAY*.

How I spent my time unplugged:

_____

_____

_____

_____

_____

_____

_____

When from our better selves
    we have too long
Been parted by the hurrying
    world, and droop,
Sick of its business, of its
    pleasures tired,
How gracious, how benign
    is Solitude.

William Wordsworth

How solitude bettered me today:

_____

_____

_____

TEXTURES THAT CENTER ME

A BIT

MORE

EVEN MORE

COMPLETELY

_____

I PERFECTLY FEEL, EVEN AT MY FINGER'S END.

John Heywood

How my senses felt alive today:

_____

_____

_____

Making a living,
economically
speaking, will be
at one with
making a life that's
worth living.

John Dewey

DATE: __/__/__

HOW MY WORK MADE MY LIFE WORTH LIVING TODAY:

_____

_____

_____

_____

_____

_____

_____

DATE: __/__/__

HOW MY LIFE MADE MY WORK WORTH DOING TODAY:

_____

_____

_____

_____

_____

_____

_____

A man's maturity consists in having found again the seriousness one had as a child, at play.

Friedrich Wilhelm Nietzsche

What I played at seriously today:

_____

_____

_____

COLORING FOCUSES ME

DO NOT STOP THINKING OF LIFE AS AN ADVENTURE.

Eleanor Roosevelt

Today's adventure:

_____

_____

_____

Leap and the net will appear.

John Burroughs

My leap today:

_____

_____

_____

My net:

_____

_____

_____

HAVING MONEY
IS RATHER LIKE
BEING A BLONDE.
IT IS MORE FUN
BUT NOT VITAL.

Mary Quant

DATE: __/__/__

WHAT IS FUN FOR ME:

_____

_____

_____

_____

_____

_____

DATE: __/__/__

WHAT IS VITAL FOR ME:

_____

_____

_____

_____

_____

_____

We can't all do everything.

Virgil

A limitation I accepted today:

_____

_____

_____

THE ONLY CERTAINTY IS THAT NOTHING IS CERTAIN.

Pliny the Elder

An uncertainty I accepted today:

_____

_____

_____

STOP
**AND SMELL
THE ROSES**

The simple things that bring me pleasure on the weekend:

_____

_____

_____

_____

_____

_____

Human felicity is produced not so much by the great pieces of good fortune that seldom happen, as by little advantages that occur every day.

Benjamin Franklin

A little advantage that occurred today:

_____

_____

_____

I dwell in Possibility—

Emily Dickinson

Today's possibility:

_____

_____

_____

All things are possible until they are proved impossible—and even the impossible may only be so as of now.

Pearl S. Buck

Something impossible that is now possible:

_____

_____

_____

DATE: __/__/__

HOW AN INCIDENT DETERMINED MY CHARACTER TODAY:

_____

_____

_____

_____

_____

_____

_____

DATE: __/__/__

HOW AN INCIDENT ILLUSTRATED MY CHARACTER TODAY:

_____

_____

_____

_____

_____

_____

What is character
but the determination
of incident?
What is incident
but the illustration
of character?

Henry James

THE ONLY RECOGNIZABLE FEATURE OF HOPE IS ACTION.

Grace Paley

How I acted on hope today:

_____

_____

_____

Action may not always bring happiness, but there is no happiness without action.

Benjamin Disraeli

An action that brought happiness today:

_____

_____

_____

S-T-R-E-T-C-H

HOW I STRETCHED MY HEART WITH A GIFT TO A FRIEND TODAY:

_____

_____

_____

_____

_____

_____

_____

DATE: __/__/__

YOUR H-E-a-R-T

HOW I STRETCHED MY HEART WITH A GIFT TO A STRANGER TODAY:

_____

_____

_____

_____

_____

_____

_____

_____

DATE: __/__/__

IF I GOT RID OF MY DEMONS, I WOULD LOSE MY ANGELS.

Tennessee Williams

My demons today:

_____

_____

_____

My angels today:

_____

_____

_____

What good is warmth without cold to give it sweetness?

John Steinbeck

The cold today:

_____

_____

_____

The warmth today:

_____

_____

_____

Success makes life easier. It doesn't make living easier.

Bruce Springsteen

DATE: __/__/__

WHAT MADE LIFE EASIER TODAY:

_____

_____

_____

_____

_____

_____

_____

DATE: __/__/__

WHAT MADE LIVING EASIER TODAY:

_____

_____

_____

_____

_____

_____

_____

I AM A CAT THAT LIKES TO GALLOP ABOUT DOING GOOD.

Stevie Smith

How I galloped about doing good today:

_____

_____

_____

Pleasure is necessarily reciprocal; no one feels [it] who does not at the same time give it. To be pleased, one must please.

Lord Chesterfield

How it pleased me to give pleasure today:

_____

_____

_____

DATE: __/__/__

BREATHE IN AND BREATHE OUT BREATHE IN AND BREATHE OUT

Sit in a chair and close your eyes.

Inhale through your nose to the count of four, and exhale slowly through pursed lips to the count of four.

Repeat this pattern as you scan your body from scalp to the bottoms of your feet.

Spend longer on areas of tension, relaxing them with your breathing.

I now feel:

_____

_____

_____

_____

_____

BREATHE IN AND BREATHE OUT BREATHE IN AND BREATHE OUT

The best things are nearest: breath in your nostrils, light in your eyes, flowers at your feet, duties at your hand.

Robert Louis Stevenson

What I found nearby today:

_____

_____

_____

THAT IS WHAT LEARNING IS. YOU SUDDENLY UNDERSTAND SOMETHING YOU'VE UNDERSTOOD ALL YOUR LIFE, BUT IN A NEW WAY.

Doris Lessing

Something I understood in a new way today:

_____

_____

_____

Cease not to learn until thou cease to live; Think that day lost wherein thou draw'st no letter To make thyself more learned, wiser, better.

Joshua Sylvester

What I did today to make myself more learned, wiser, better:

_____

_____

_____

DATE: __/__/__

WHAT I WATCHED TODAY:

_____

_____

_____

_____

_____

_____

_____

DATE: __/__/__

WHAT I OBSERVED TODAY:

_____

_____

_____

_____

_____

_____

_____

YOU CAN OBSERVE A LOT BY WATCHING.

Yogi Berra

NATURE THAT CENTERS ME

A BIT

MORE

EVEN MORE

COMPLETELY

_____

In the spring, at the end of the day, you should smell like dirt.

Margaret Atwood

How I grounded myself today:

_____

_____

_____

DATE: __/__/__

A PART OF KINDNESS CONSISTS IN LOVING PEOPLE MORE THAN THEY DESERVE.

Joseph Joubert

Whom I loved today more than they deserve:

_____

_____

Why?

_____

_____

Kindness expiates a multitude of sins.

Anonymous

My sin:

_____

_____

How I expiated it with kindness:

_____

_____

Life shrinks or expands in proportion to one's courage.

Anaïs Nin

DATE: __/__/__

MY LIFE SHRANK TODAY BECAUSE I LACKED THE COURAGE TO:

_____

_____

_____

_____

_____

_____

_____

DATE: __/__/__

MY LIFE EXPANDED TODAY BECAUSE I HAD THE COURAGE TO:

_____

_____

_____

_____

_____

_____

The motto of all the mongoose family is "Run and find out."

Rudyard Kipling

What I found out today:

_____

_____

_____

DATE: __/__/__

IT IS BETTER TO KNOW NOTHING THAN TO KNOW WHAT AIN'T SO.

Josh Billings

I now know this ain't so:

_____

_____

So I:

_____

_____

MY FITNESS GOAL
and how I will get there

GOAL

START

Fitness is not about being better than someone else.... It is about being better than you used to be.

Brett Hoebel

I used to only be able to:

_____

_____

Now I can:

_____

_____

LIFE IS NOT A POPULARITY CONTEST. BE BRAVE, TAKE THE HILL, BUT FIRST ANSWER THE QUESTION, "WHAT IS MY HILL?"

Matthew McConaughey

What my hill is today:

_____

_____

_____

IF YOU ALWAYS DO WHAT INTERESTS YOU, AT LEAST ONE PERSON IS PLEASED.

Katharine Hepburn

I was pleased today when I:

_____

_____

_____

DATE: __/__/__

WHAT MY FRIENDS AND I LIKE:

_____

_____

_____

_____

_____

_____

_____

DATE: __/__/__

WHAT MY FRIENDS AND I DISLIKE:

_____

_____

_____

_____

_____

_____

_____

To like and dislike the same things, that is indeed true friendship.

Sallust

A little learning is a dangerous thing; Drink deep, or taste not the Pierian spring.

Alexander Pope

What I learned from drinking deeply today:

_____

_____

_____

DATE: __/__/__

There is no passion to be found in playing small—in settling for a life that is less than the one you are capable of living.

Nelson Mandela

How I played large today:

_____

_____

_____

The manner of giving is worth more than the gift.

Pierre Corneille

The priceless way I gave a gift today:

_____

_____

_____

DATE: __/__/__

to: _____

_____

_____

Thank You!

for

_____

_____

_____

_____

_____

_____

_____

EVERYTHING THAT IRRITATES US ABOUT OTHERS CAN LEAD US TO AN UNDERSTANDING OF OURSELVES.

Carl Gustav Jung

What irritated me today:

_____

_____

What I learned about myself from that:

_____

_____

IF YOU WANT TO GO FAST, GO ALONE. IF YOU WANT TO GO FAR, GO TOGETHER.

African proverb

How far we went together today:

_____

_____

_____

Knowing is
not enough;
we must apply.
Willing is
not enough,
we must do.

Johann Wolfgang von Goethe

DATE: __/__/__

HOW I APPLIED MY KNOWLEDGE TODAY:

_____

_____

_____

_____

_____

_____

_____

DATE: __/__/__

HOW I ACTED ON MY WILLINGNESS TODAY:

_____

_____

_____

_____

_____

_____

_____

YOUR TIME IS LIMITED, SO DON'T WASTE IT LIVING SOMEONE ELSE'S LIFE.

Steve Jobs

How I lived my life in my own way today:

_____

_____

_____

You must begin to think of yourself as becoming the person you want to be.

David Viscott

How I am becoming the person I want to be:

_____

_____

_____

TURN OFF / IGNORE / HIDE ALL ELECTRONIC DEVICES FOR *A WEEKEND*.

How I spent my time unplugged:

_____

_____

_____

_____

_____

_____

_____

_____

_____

Thought works in silence, so does virtue. One might erect statues to Silence.

Thomas Carlyle

How I honored silence today:

_____

_____

_____

DATE: __/__/__

IF YOU THINK ADVENTURE IS DANGEROUS, TRY ROUTINE— IT'S LETHAL.

Paulo Coelho

How I avoided routine today:

_____

_____

_____

ADVENTURES THAT CENTER ME

A BIT

MORE

EVEN MORE

COMPLETELY

_____

He has achieved success who has lived well, laughed often, and loved much.

Bessie Anderson Stanley

DATE: __/__/__

HOW LIVING WELL LED TO SUCCESS TODAY:

_____

_____

_____

DATE: __/__/__

HOW LAUGHING OFTEN LED TO SUCCESS TODAY:

_____

_____

_____

DATE: __/__/__

HOW LOVING MUCH LED TO SUCCESS TODAY:

_____

_____

_____

You have your colors, you have your brushes. Paint paradise and walk right in.

Nikos Kazantzakis

How I painted my paradise today:

_____

_____

_____

The highest form of wisdom is kindness.

The Talmud

What I learned by being kind today:

_____

_____

_____

My happiness is to increase other people's. To be happy myself I need the happiness of all.

André Gide

How I increased the happiness of others today:

_____

_____

_____

DATE: _/_/_

WHATEVER YOU'RE MEANT TO DO, DO IT NOW. THE CONDITIONS ARE ALWAYS IMPOSSIBLE.

Doris Lessing

What I will do today:

_____

_____

_____

The further I get, the further I want to go.

Nas

Where I want to go today:

_____

_____

_____

Copyright © 2016 by **ROBIE LLC**.

All rights reserved.

Published in the United States by **CLARKSON POTTER/PUBLISHERS**, an imprint of the
CROWN PUBLISHING GROUP, a division of **PENGUIN RANDOM HOUSE LLC**, New York.

crownpublishing.com
clarksonpotter.com

CLARKSON POTTER is a trademark and **POTTER** with colophon
is a registered trademark of **PENGUIN RANDOM HOUSE LLC**.

Four stretching exercises from *A Guide to Basic Stretches* used by
permission of the **MAYO FOUNDATION FOR MEDICAL EDUCATION AND RESEARCH**
(pages 78, 79, 258, 259).

Patterns © Fine Art Studio | Shutterstock.com (pages 22, 52, 83, 126, 156, 203,
246, 270, 315, 360); © Hardia999 | Dreamstime.com—Stylized Roses Seamless
Pattern Photo (pages 49, 108, 169, 229, 289, 349)

ISBN 978-0-553-45970-8

Printed in China

2 4 6 8 10 9 7 5 3 1

CONCEIVED AND COMPILED by Dian G. Smith and Robie Rogge
COVER by Danielle Deschenes
INTERIOR DESIGN by Lana Le

First Edition